LET'S FIND OUT! PLANTS

HOW PLANTS REPRODUCE

JUDY SILVERSTEIN GRAY

Britannica Educational Publishing

IN ASSOCIATION WITH

ROSEN EDUCATIONAL SERVICES

Published in 2019 by Britannica Educational Publishing (a trademark of Encyclopædia Britannica, Inc.) in association with The Rosen Publishing Group, Inc.
29 East 21st Street, New York, NY 10010

Distributed exclusively by Rosen Publishing.
To see additional Britannica Educational Publishing titles, go to rosenpublishing.com.

First Edition

Britannica Educational Publishing
J.E. Luebering: Executive Director, Core Editorial
Mary Rose McCudden: Editor, Britannica Student Encyclopedia

Rosen Publishing
Bailey Maxim: Editor
Nelson Sá: Art Director
Nicole Russo-Duca: Series Designer/Book Layout
Cindy Reiman: Photography Manager
Ellina Litmanovich: Photo Researcher

Library of Congress Cataloging-in-Publication Data

Names: Gray, Judy Silverstein, author.
Title: How plants reproduce / Judy Silverstein Gray.
Description: New York : Britannica Educational Publishing, in Association with Rosen Educational Services, 2019. | Series: Let's find out! Plants | Audience: Grades 1-4. | Includes bibliographical references and index.
Identifiers: LCCN 2017055340| ISBN 9781538301937 (library bound) | ISBN 9781538301944 (pbk.) | ISBN 9781538301951 (6 pack)
Subjects: LCSH: Plants—Reproduction—Juvenile literature. | Seeds—Juvenile literature. | Pollination—Juvenile literature. | Growth (Plants—Juvenile literature.
Classification: LCC QK825 .G73 2019 | DDC 575.6--dc23
LC record available at https://lccn.loc.gov/2017055340

Manufactured in the United States of America

Photo credits: Cover, interior pages background TIF Fotos/Shutterstock.com; p. 4 © PeJo/Fotolia; p. 5 © Profotokris/Fotolia; p. 6 Achiichiii/Shutterstock.com; p. 7 Likit Supasai/Shutterstock.com; pp. 8, 9, 11, 22, 24 © Encyclopædia Britannica, Inc.; p. 10 © Thomas C. Boyden; p. 12 Roman Samokhin/Shutterstock.com; p. 13 © William Whitehurst/Corbis; p. 14 USDA Forest Service; p. 15 Fomin Serhii/Shutterstock.com; p. 16 EstrellaBuena/Shutterstock.com; p. 17 Wojciech Tchorzewski/Shutterstock.com; p. 18 Henrik Larsson/Fotolia; p. 19 © J. Ziffer/1978; p. 20 Jiang Hongyan/Shutterstock.com; p. 21 A to Z Botanical Collection/Encyclopædia Britannica, Inc.; p. 23 © Sydney Karp–Photo/Nats; p. 25 AdstockRF; p. 26 Corepics VOF/Shutterstock.com; p. 27 © Michael Van Woert/NOAA NESDIS, ORA; p. 28 © G. Fahnenstiel/NOAA, Great Lakes Environmental Research Laboratory; p. 29 csp/Shutterstock.com.

Contents

Plants on Our Planet

Plants are living things found in just about every place on Earth. Like little factories, they make their own food. In fact, they provide most of the food animals and humans eat. They also provide the oxygen we breathe.

Plants start life as tiny plants. Then they grow into adulthood and **reproduce**, and, later, they die. Botanists

The life cycle of a carrot plant is two years. During the second year, it produces flowers and seeds.

(scientists who study plants) classify plants by how they reproduce. Plants make more of their kind either by seeds or by spores. Seeds and spores are small structures that develop on plants and then fall off. They then may grow into new plants. Seeds are larger and more complex than spores. Most plants begin from seeds and have roots, stems, and leaves. The roots grow downward, spreading out into the soil to soak up water and minerals. They also anchor the plant in place. The stem develops and grows, holding the plant upright.

VOCABULARY

To **reproduce** is to make more living things of the same species to continue a species.

A nut is a dry, hard fruit that contains one seed. Many of the foods that people think of as nuts, such as peanuts and almonds, are not true nuts.

Roots and Shoots

Vascular plants are one kind of plant. Vascular plants mostly reproduce using seeds. They have special tissues called xylem and phloem. The tissues form a tubelike transport system within the plants. The xylem carries nutrients and water from the roots to the leaves, even in the tallest redwood trees. The phloem transports water and sugars from the leaves to other parts of the plant. Vascular plants are able to grow to be large and tall.

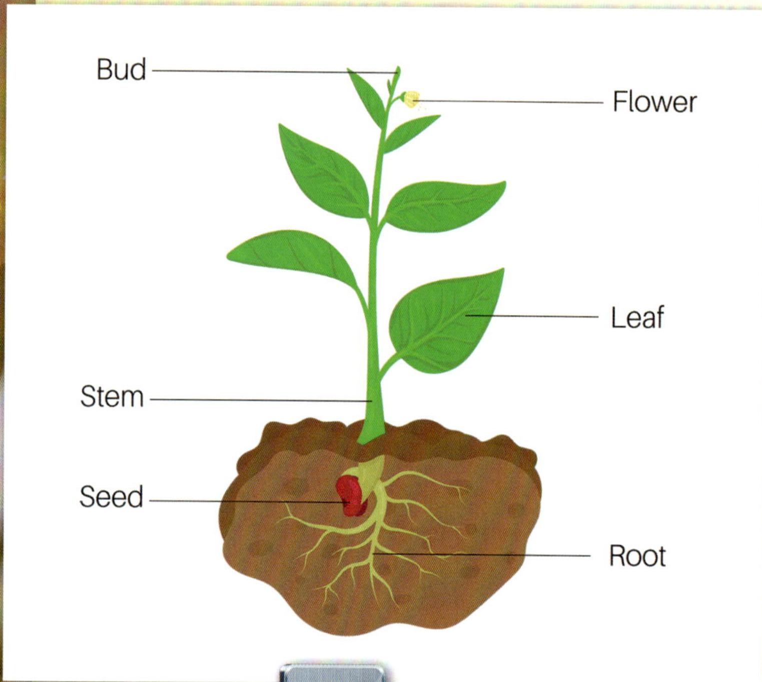

Water travels from the roots to the other parts of a plant via the xylem and phloem tissues inside the plant.

Mosses are small, seedless plants that often grow in moist, shady places.

Nonvascular plants are much smaller because they do not have true roots and stems, which support vascular plants and hold them up tall. Instead, they spread out, absorbing water and minerals directly from the air, ground, rocks, or trees. Mosses are nonvascular plants. They get fed by soaking up water and minerals from the ground and air, like a sponge.

COMPARE AND CONTRAST

What are some differences between vascular and nonvascular plants?

Growing Up

Many vascular plants are flowering plants. Another name for them is angiosperms. The flowers of these plants produce seeds. The seed is made after a structure called an ovule, an egg cell, receives pollen. The pollen gives the ovule the rest of the material it needs to become a seed. This process is called fertilization.

There are two ways angiosperms can be fertilized. Some flowering plants have both male and female parts, which are

A plant can pollinate itself if it has both male and female parts, called stamens and pistils.

Self-pollination

called the stamen and the pistil. They have all the parts they need, so they transfer pollen from their own stamens to their pistils. This is called self-pollination. The other way is called cross-pollination, which means that the pollen has to come from another plant of the same kind.

THINK ABOUT IT

How do you think pollen might get from one plant to another?

Most plants depend on a carrier, such as a bee, to bring pollen to them from another plant.

Flowers and Fruit

Water lily plants produce a fruit that has seeds inside. When the fruit opens, the seeds sink or float away to produce new plants.

Angiosperms have seeds and fruit. Both seeds and fruit play a part in reproduction. Each seed contains its own food supply and an embryo, a tiny structure that can grow into another plant. For the seed to grow into a new plant, it must have the right amount of moisture and be kept at the right temperatures.

When the conditions are right, the seed coat (a protective covering) is dampened and the embryo expands. It bursts open and begins growing

Think About It

Sunflowers make between eight hundred and two thousand seeds. Do you think this large number of seeds helps the sunflowers reproduce successfully?

upward to reach the sunlight it needs to make its own food and develop. The embryo uses its own food source until it becomes a big enough plant to make its own. Other parts of the embryo grow downward to form the plant's roots.

The seed of a corn plant is called a kernel. It has an embryo inside it.

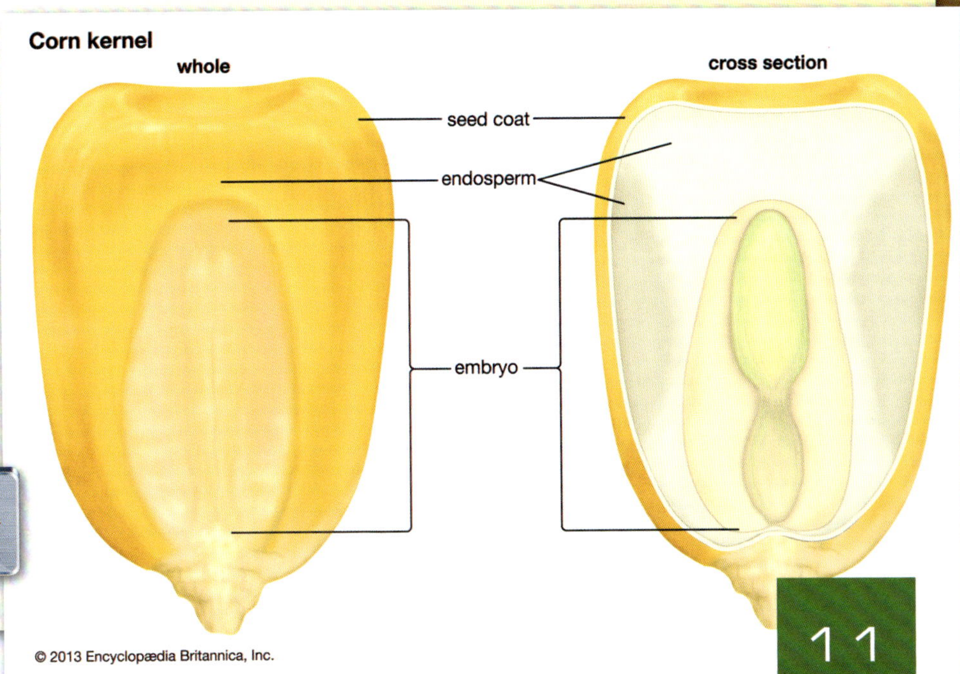

After a flower is pollinated, the ovules, inside a part of the plant called the ovary, begin changing into seeds. The flower's petals may start falling off. As the ovary swells and grows larger, it eventually becomes the fruit. The fruit provides protection for the seeds inside.

Different fruits develop seeds differently. They store their seeds in different places. Cherries and peaches have only one seed, inside the fruit.

Apples have their seeds on the inside. Often you can see a seed or two when the apple is cut in half.

This one large seed is called the stone or pit. In apples, the ovary and the seeds become the core of the fruit. Pomegranates have hundreds of seeds encased in fleshy sections of the fruit. Strawberries have their seeds on the outside of the fruit. They look like dots on the flesh.

Think About It

Why does a plant need to protect its seeds?

The peas that people eat are the seeds of the pea plant. They grow inside what is called a pod. The pod breaks open when the peas are ripe.

Vascular Plants with Cones

Another type of vascular plant is called a conifer. Conifers are a group of trees and shrubs that produce cones instead of flowers or fruits. The cones carry their seeds.

Most conifers are evergreens, or trees that keep their leaves year-round. Their thin leaves are usually called

Conifers are found in all parts of the world where trees grow. They are most abundant in cool regions.

Cycads have grown on Earth for millions of years. They look similar to palms, but they are not closely related.

needles. The cones grow on the tree's branches.

Conifers include some of the tallest and oldest living plants on our planet. There are more than 550 types. Fir trees, redwoods, cedars, junipers, and spruce are evergreen conifers. Cycads are another type of plant that grows cones, but they are not classified as conifers.

VOCABULARY

Cycads are large, woody plants that look like palms.

Reproduction in Conifers

Some types of conifer grow male and female cones on the same tree. Others have male or female cones on separate trees. The male cones, which are smaller than female cones, produce pollen.

The larger cones that drop off the tree and can be seen on the forest floor are the female cones. They

People are familiar with the large female pine cones that fall off a conifer. Both male and female cones are needed for reproduction.

have an embryo. They also have a protective covering that becomes the seed coat.

Compare and Contrast

How are fruits and cones different? How are they alike?

Wind carries pollen to the female cones. When the female cones receive the pollen they develop seeds under the scales. The female cones have woody and sticky scales that hold the seeds in place. The scales slowly open until the seeds fall out. Wind or animals carry the seeds to spots where new conifers can grow.

The seeds of a conifer can be seen inside a cone if it is cut open.

Plants with Spores

Many plants reproduce by spores. Spores are most common in seedless plants, but they act like seeds. Spores can be found on the underside of leaves or at the top of a plant's stalk. Ferns are one common kind of plant that has spores. Others

Think About It

Ferns are often called a "pioneer species" since they were the first plants to settle, survive, and grow on Earth. How do you think their way of reproducing helped that happen?

The liverwort's name comes from its shape, which in some varieties looks like that of the human liver.

Hornworts are small nonvascular plants with spores. They usually grow on damp soils or on rocks in tropical and warm regions.

are liverworts and mosses. To reproduce, the parent plant sheds or releases its spores into the environment. Once released, the spores do not produce a new plant right away. They develop into a structure that produces female and male cells. A female and a male cell must unite to form a zygote. Sometimes the male and female spores are on the same plant. Often, though, the spores for the zygote must come from different plants. If the zygote develops in the right environment, it will grow into a new spore-producing plant.

Vegetative Reproduction

Many kinds of plants reproduce asexually. That means that they have structures that can make a new individual without special male and female cells. Instead, they reproduce by making exact copies of themselves. One kind of asexual reproduction is called vegetative reproduction. In vegetative reproduction, a new plant may grow from a piece of the parent plant. Another way it can happen is if the new plant grows from a special structure. Potato plants have seeds, for example, but usually grow from the tuber. The tuber is the part of the

If potatoes are left in the pantry too long, they may start to sprout buds.

VOCABULARY

Horizontal means level with the horizon, or running right to left rather than up or down.

plant that we eat. Strawberries have seeds, too, but they also put out runners, which creep along the ground and can grow into new plants.

Vegetative reproduction happens through plant organs called rhizomes, corms, stolons, and bulbs, in addition to runners and tubers. These are all different kinds of stems. Rhizomes are fleshy, horizontal stems that grow underground and cause the plant to multiply. Tubers are also fleshy stems that

Leaves sprout from the top of a strawberry plant.

This chart shows several different methods of plant reproduction.

usually grow underground. Their buds can develop into new individuals. Corms are bulblike stems. They also grow underground and can grow structures that become new plants.

Vegetative reproduction comes with a risk. If plants reproduce by making exact copies of themselves, all

Compare and Contrast

What are some advantages and disadvantages to vegetative reproduction?

the plants of that kind in a certain area will be just like each other. If a disease attacks the plants, it can kill them all because none of them has any advantage over the others to protect it.

Farmers rely on vegetative reproduction because it lets crops increase quickly. As we have seen, plants that reproduce this way are identical to the parent plant. Because such plants in the same community are very much alike, these crops look or taste the same as each other.

Kalanchoe plants have colorful flowers. They are easy to grow from stem or leaf cuttings.

Special Kinds of Plant Reproduction

In another kind of asexual reproduction, called apomixis, a plant develops seeds that are not male or female, and they can develop without pollination. The new plants are exactly like the parent plant.

Blackberry plants sometimes use apomixis to reproduce. When unfertilized seeds from blackberry plants fall off the

A dandelion blossom is really a bouquet of many flowers. An individual flower is shown in the middle.

parent plant, they germinate and grow into adult plants. Since the plant does not have to wait for fertilization to occur, it begins to grow quickly.

Some plants alternate sexual and asexual reproduction. This is called agamospermy. It means plants have more than one way to make more plants. For example, during one season, a fern's spores will go through a life cycle without needing fertilization. The next time the plant reproduces, it will use the fertilization process.

VOCABULARY

The word **agamospermy** comes from words meaning "unmarried seed."

Roses are a common flower that have multiple ways of reproducing.

When Reproduction Fails

Reproduction in nature is usually well-coordinated. Sometimes, though, it just does not work. There are many reasons that plants fail to reproduce.

An egg may be difficult to fertilize. To form seeds, a flower's stigma needs the right amount of pollen. Plants also need the right amount of light, heat, and moisture to reproduce. In **clonal**

Botanists often work in greenhouses, where they can grow plants that are not native to the area.

communities, plants can be too similar to each other to reproduce successfully. They may produce flowers but not enough fruit. When fertilization fails, seeds will not form.

Botanists study plants to understand how their environment helps or hurts their ability to reproduce. They help to develop plants that can live through droughts and heat waves. Even though scientists can develop new plants, they cannot be sure that those new plants will always reproduce successfully.

Vocabulary

Clonal communities are groups of plants that are identical copies of the parent plants.

Very few plants can survive in the cold conditions of the Arctic or Antarctica.

The More Things Change

Millions of years ago, making spores was the only way for the earliest plants to reproduce. In today's world, plants produce seeds and flowers in addition to spores. They have also evolved to use vegetative reproduction. Over these millions of years, plants have become much more diverse, and there is a greater chance for plant species to survive. Plants have developed different ways to reproduce. Some have fruit and flowers that need to be pollinated. Some have lost their ability to reproduce sexually and

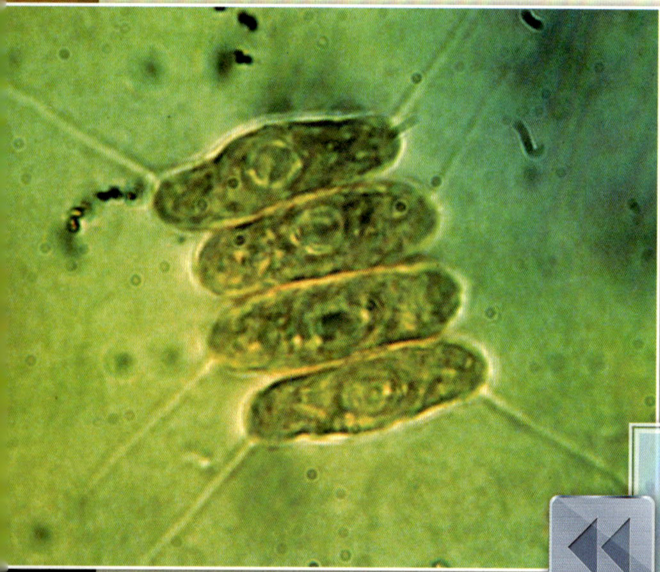

Scientists have discovered that green algae probably gave rise to land plants millions of years ago.

can only make identical copies of themselves. Still other plants alternate their methods of reproduction. By studying how plants adapt and develop reproductive techniques, botanists can better understand what conditions are best for plants to survive and increase.

Think About It

Do you think having different ways to make new plants might be important for plant species? Why or why not?

The plants you see in a garden or park reproduce and grow using many different methods.

Glossary

angiosperm A flowering plant.

conifer Mostly evergreen trees and shrubs that have cones and grow leaves resembling needles.

drought A long time, usually months or years, in which there is no rain.

embryo A tiny young plant inside a seed.

fertilization The combining of male and female cells to make a new living thing such as a plant.

germinate To begin to sprout or evolve.

moss A classification of plants that have no flowers and grow in patches like carpets clinging to rocks, bark, or damp ground.

ovary The part of the flower that becomes a fruit.

oxygen A chemical that is found in the air. It has no color, taste, or smell, and it is necessary for life.

phloem Tissue that carries dissolved food and sugars throughout the plant.

pollen A sticky powder formed in flowers.

pollinate To move pollen to the ovary of a flower and fertilize its female sex cells.

sexual reproduction Reproduction through combining male and female parts.

spore A plant structure made up of a cell that is capable of producing a new plant.

stigma The top part in the center of a flower that receives pollen.

vascular Of or relating to a tube or channel for carrying a fluid.

vessels Thin, tube-shaped passages that carry fluids.

xylem Tissue that carries water and dissolved materials upward and that usually makes up the woody parts of a plant.

zygote A fertilized egg.

For More Information

Books

Bishop, Celeste. *Why Do Plants Have Fruits?* New York, NY: PowerKids Press, 2016.

Carr, Aaron. *Plants*. New York, NY: Av2 by Weigl Publishers, 2013.

Heddle, Rebecca. *Plants, Pollen and Pollinators*. London, UK: HarperCollins, 2016.

Schafer, Lola M., Adam Schaefer, and Frann Preston-Gannon. *Because of an Acorn*. San Francisco, CA: Chronicle Books, 2016.

Senker, Cath. *Plant Reproduction: How Do You Grow a Giant Pumpkin?* Hampshire, UK: Raintree Press, 2014.

Strauss, Rochelle, and M. Thompson. *Tree of Life: The Incredible Biodiversity of Life on Earth*. Toronto, ON, and Tonowanda, NY: Kids Can Press, 2013.

Waldron, Melanie. *Plants*. Chicago, IL: Heinemann Library, 2014.

Websites

Bees Matter
http://www.beesmatter.ca/plant-reproduction-and-the-role-of- honey -bees

National Geographic Kids
https://www.natgeokids.com/za/discover/science/nature/the-life-cycle-of-flowering-plants
Twitter: @NGKids, Facebook: @nationalgeographickids

Science Learning Hub
https://www.sciencelearn.org.nz/resources/100-plant-reproduction
Twitter, Facebook: @NZScienceLearn

INDEX